The Primary Source Library of Famous Explorers™

Juan Ponce de León
A Primary Source Biography

Lynn Hoogenboom

The Rosen Publishing Group's

PowerKids Press™
PRIMARY SOURCE

New York

For Ari

Published in 2006 by The Rosen Publishing Group, Inc.
29 East 21st Street, New York, NY 10010

Copyright © 2006 by The Rosen Publishing Group, Inc.

First Edition

Editor: Daryl Heller
Book Design: Albert B. Hanner
Layout Design: Greg Tucker
Photo Researcher: Gabriel Caplan

Photo Credits: Cover, p. 5 (top) © Bettmann/Corbis; p. 5 (map) by Greg Tucker; p. 6 (left) Art Resource, NY; pp. 6 (right), 16 (bottom), 21 The New York Public Library/Art Resource, NY; p. 9 Office of Underwater Science, Indiana University; p. 9 (bottom) Bibliotheque Nationale, Paris, France, Giraudon/Bridgeman Art Library; p. 10 (top) © North Wind Picture Archives; p. 10 (bottom) © Corbis; p. 12 (top) Bildarchiv Preussischer Kulturbesitz/Art Resource, NY; pp. 12 (bottom), 15 (top) Archivo General de Indias, Sevilla; p. 12 Patronato 198, ramo 1, p. 15 Indiferente General 418, libro III, folios 253–254; p. 15 (bottom) The Art Archive; p. 16 (top) NOAA Central Library; p. 19 (top) Erich Lessing/Art Resource, NY; p. 19 (bottom) The Granger Collection, New York.

Library of Congress Cataloging-in-Publication Data

Hoogenboom, Lynn.
Juan Ponce de León : a primary source biography / Lynn Hoogenboom.
p. cm. — (The primary source library of famous explorers) Includes index.
ISBN 1-4042-3040-8 (library binding)
1. Ponce de León, Juan, 1460?–1521—Juvenile literature. 2. Explorers—America—Biography—Juvenile literature. 3. Explorers—Spain—Biography—Juvenile literature. 4. America—Discovery and exploration—Spanish—Juvenile literature. I. Title.
E125.P7H66 2006
970.01'6'092—dc22   515 894 9

2005007018

Manufactured in the United States of America

Contents

Early Years

Most of what we know about the explorer Juan Ponce de León comes from a Spanish historian, Antonio de Herrera, who wrote about Ponce de León 80 years after his death. Herrera may have seen a journal written by Ponce de León or one of the men who sailed with him.

Ponce de León was born around 1474, in Tervas de San Campos, Spain. His parents were **nobles**. Luis Ponce de León was his father. His mother was Leonor de Figueroa. As a boy Ponce de León was a **page** to Pedro Núñez de Guzmán, who was an important person at the royal **court**. Ponce de León later served as a soldier.

In 1492, Christopher Columbus became the first European to discover America. Columbus returned to Spain in 1493 to report his discovery to Ferdinand and Isabella, who were the king and queen of Spain. On September 25, 1493, Columbus set sail on his second **voyage**, with 17 ships and about 1,200 sailors, soldiers, and **settlers**. One of the soldiers was Ponce de León.

Because Ponce de León's parents were nobles, he was allowed to be a page at the royal court. A page tended to a nobleman's food and clothes. In return the page would be educated and taught the skills required of a soldier.

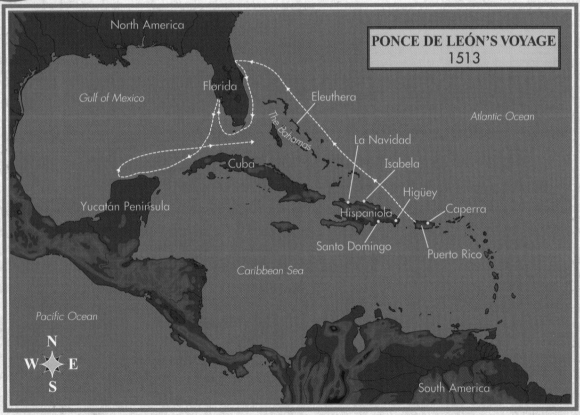

North America

PONCE DE LEÓN'S VOYAGE
1513

Gulf of Mexico

Florida

Eleuthera

The Bahamas

Atlantic Ocean

La Navidad

Cuba

Isabela

Higüey

Yucatán Peninsula

Caperra

Hispaniola

Santo Domingo

Puerto Rico

Caribbean Sea

Pacific Ocean

N
W   E
S

South America

In 1513, the Spanish king gave Juan Ponce de León permission to search for a land called Bimini. Ponce de León sailed from Puerto Rico, a Spanish colony, in March 1513 with three ships. After exploring the coastal areas of Florida, they sailed southwest. By June 26, the ships reached southern Mexico. Ponce de León then sailed east and reached the island of Eleuthera on August 18, 1513.

5

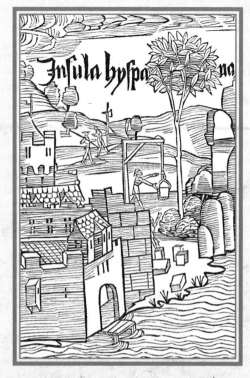

This is a picture of La Navidad, a fort that Christopher Columbus built on his first visit to Hispaniola in late 1492. When Columbus returned to La Navidad in November 1493, he found that the fort had been burned. The men he had left behind at La Navidad had been killed.

A German artist made this 1505 picture of Native Americans. In the background are the ships of the European explorers.

The New World

In early 1494, Columbus set up a second colony in what Europeans called the New World. The colony was on an island he called Hispaniola. Today this island is divided between Haiti and the Dominican Republic. The colonists that Columbus brought from Spain were not used to the hot weather. Many of them got sick. Most of them did not plan to do any work. They hoped to get rich by finding gold. When Columbus told the colonists he would not give them food unless they worked, the colonists became angry. They stole food from the Taíno Indians, who lived on Hispaniola. The colonists also kidnapped Taínos and forced the Taínos to work for them as slaves.

At some point some of the ships sailed back to Spain, with many of the settlers. Juan Ponce de León seems to have been one of those who left. The only reason historians know that Ponce de León left Hispaniola is because there are records of him sailing again to Hispaniola in 1502.

Hispaniola

In February 1502, Nicolás de Ovando sailed to Hispaniola with 30 ships to **replace** Columbus as governor. Juan Ponce de León was on one of the ships. Shortly after Ponce de León arrived at Hispaniola he married Leonor, the daughter of an innkeeper on the island. The couple had three daughters, Juana, Isabel, and Maria, and one son, Luis.

The Spaniards had not **conquered** the Taíno Indians in Higüey, in eastern Hispaniola. In 1503, Governor Ovando sent Juan de Esquivel to fight the Taínos. Ponce de León went with him as a soldier. The Spaniards won easily because they had better weapons and used large dogs to attack the Taínos. Esquivel left some soldiers behind in a small **fort**. After the Taínos burned the fort in 1504, Esquivel and 400 men went to fight them. Ponce de León was one of Esquivel's **lieutenants**. The **campaign** ended in a **massacre**. Even after the Spaniards won the battle, they continued to kill the Taínos.

This cave painting from the early 1500s was done by Taíno Indians in Hispaniola. Historians have tried to interpret, or explain, the story being told in this painting. Historians think that a Taíno chief is watching as bread is prepared for the Spanish conquerors. The bread is baked over a fire and is then sent to the Spanish by boat.

The Spanish brought dogs and horses to the New World. Both animals were used to chase and attack the Indians. Around 1502, the Taíno Indians in Higüey attacked the Spanish after one of the Spaniards' dogs killed an Indian.

The settlers who returned to Spain from Hispaniola said bad things about Christopher Columbus. King Ferdinand and Queen Isabella sent a royal commissioner, Francisco de Bobadilla, to Hispaniola to investigate, or find more information. Bobadilla arrested Columbus and sent him back to Spain in chains. Nicolás de Ovando became the new governor of Hispaniola.

This 1572 picture Bananas and Other Fruit Trees of Hispaniola was based on an earlier drawing by Girolamo Benzoni. Banana trees, which grow on some of the Caribbean Islands, were exotic to Europeans. Exotic means something that is from another country and is often thought to be strange and unusual. Platano is the Spanish word for "banana," and it is written on the bottom-right side of the picture.

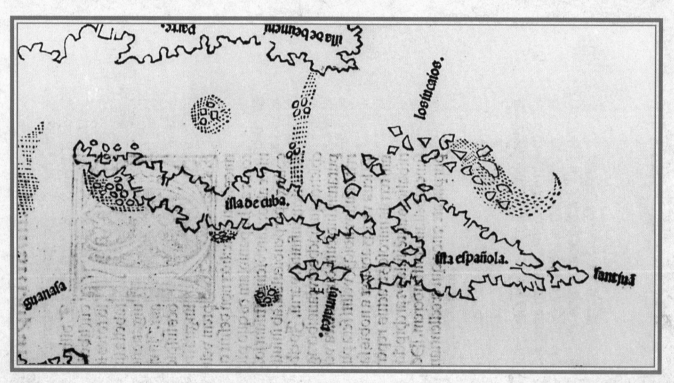

This is a close-up of the Caribbean Islands from Peter Martyr's 1511 map of the New World. Peter Martyr was an Italian historian who worked in the Spanish court of King Charles V. Martyr's map includes labels for Isla de Cuba, Española, and the Isla de Beimeni. These areas were later known as Cuba and Hispaniola. The Isla de Beimini, or Bimini, as it was most often spelled, was an unexplored area to the north that Peter Martyr, the mapmaker, believed was there.

New Challenges

Because he had helped **defeat** the Taínos, Juan Ponce de León was named **frontier** governor of Higüey. He was given about 225 acres (91 ha) in the area, where he raised yucca, sweet potatoes, pigs, cattle, and horses. Ponce de León was also given Indian slaves to work the land. Ponce de León's farm was a financial success because ships going to Europe would often stop there for supplies.

Ponce de León heard there was gold on the nearby island of Puerto Rico, east of Hispaniola. Governor Ovando could not give Ponce de León permission to colonize Puerto Rico, though. Another man already had permission until 1507. However, Ovando said he would not stop Ponce de León from trying. On June 24, 1506, five boats carrying 100 men landed at the mouth of the Añasco River in Puerto Rico. Ponce de León did some exploring and began building a town that was named Caparra, located close to modern-day San Juan.

When the Spanish colonists came to Puerto Rico, the Taíno Indians thought the Spaniards were immortal. If someone is immortal, he or she will live forever. To test this idea, the Taíno caught a Spaniard in 1510 and drowned him. When he did not come back to life, the Taíno in Puerto Rico knew that the Spanish could be killed.

From the First Relation of Gold

"The first relation of the gold that was first melted in this island of San Juan by order of Juan Ponce de León, governor of such island, and of the gold that belonged to his highness, for reason of the quinto."

This means that Ponce de León, San Juan's governor, was in charge of giving shares of the first batch of melted gold to the colonists. The first person to receive the gold was the Spanish king, called his highness. He was sent one-fifth of all the gold.

This 1510 report explained how the gold found on San Juan Island, or Puerto Rico, was given away after it had been melted down. The Spanish king received a quinto, or one fifth, of any gold that was found or taken on San Juan. This was an early name for Puerto Rico.

12

Governor of Puerto Rico

Juan Ponce de León got official royal permission to start his colony in Puerto Rico on June 15, 1508. In August he returned to Puerto Rico. The Taínos in Puerto Rico had heard what had happened to the Taínos in Hispaniola. Most of them decided not to fight the Spanish, however. Although the Spanish still enslaved the Taínos of Puerto Rico, they were not treated as poorly as the Taínos of Hispaniola. Ponce de León became Puerto Rico's first governor. He was honest and most people found him to be fair and good at his job.

In the first few years after the Spanish arrived, many of the Taínos in Puerto Rico caught **diseases** from the Spaniards and died. As the number of Indians on Puerto Rico decreased, the number of Spaniards who wanted Indians to work for them went up. The Spaniards began making more and more **demands** on the Taínos. In 1511, the Taínos **revolted**. After fighting many battles, the Taínos were defeated later that same year.

The Discovery of Florida

Early explorers usually got **grants** from kings that promised the explorer a share of the money made in any lands they discovered. Sometimes the grants would allow the explorers to rule colonies in those new lands. Christopher Columbus was given such a grant before he discovered America. In 1511, the Council of Castile in Spain ruled that the grant gave Columbus's son, Diego, the right to govern the lands that his father had discovered. Nicolás de Ovando had appointed Juan Ponce de León governor of Puerto Rico. Because Ovando had been an enemy of Diego's father, Diego did not want Ponce de León to be governor.

King Ferdinand asked that Ponce de León explore Bimini, the land north of Hispaniola, where he could start a colony and search for the **Fountain of Youth** that was said to be there. On March 3, 1513, Ponce de León sailed from Puerto Rico with three ships. On April 2, they landed on the eastern coast of Florida, not far from modern-day Daytona Beach. He named the land La Florida, "the flowered one."

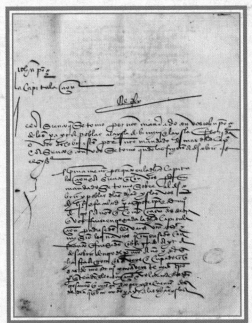

From the First Capitulation for Discovery of Bimini

"Our Officials who reside in the Island of Española: Juan Ponce de León wrote me that which you will see, by the letter which goes with this, upon the settlement of an Island which is called Binyny. I have commanded reply that we have committed this business to him and ye will take the agreement that must be taken."

Ponce de León had asked for royal permission to explore Bimini, spelled "Binyny" above. The king gave his consent. The king told his officials in Hispaniola that he had authorized Ponce de León's trip to Bimini.

This is the first page of the First Capitulation for Discovery of Bimini. The capitulation, or agreement, was authorized by Ferdinand, king of Spain, on February 23, 1512. Although Ponce de León did not find Bimini, he did find Florida.

This is a close-up from the cover of a 1700s Spanish history book. Juan Ponce de León is pictured in the lower right corner. Three of his ships are shown sailing from Puerto Rico to search for the island of Bimini. On this 1513 trip, Ponce de León discovered Florida, which he thought was a large island.

This 1678 chart by Athanasius Kircher was the first printed drawing of the ocean currents that Ponce de León discovered in 1513. The darker areas stand for the Gulf Stream, or the warm ocean currents that flow quickly north and east along the coast of North America. Even today sailors and scientists continue to study and chart the Gulf Stream.

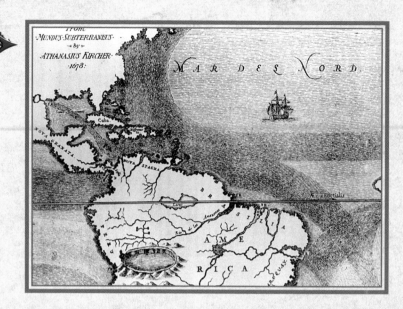

The Indians of Puerto Rico, Hispaniola, and Cuba told the Spanish about a fountain that would make old people young again. The magic took place once a person sipped water from the fountain. This fountain was thought to be on Bimini, an island in the modern-day Bahamas. Ponce de León never found the Fountain of Youth.

The Gulf Stream

After discovering Florida Ponce de León explored its coast. As he sailed south, he ran into a water current so strong that it drove the ships backward. Ponce de León had discovered the Gulf Stream, a powerful ocean current that begins in the Gulf of Mexico, then travels north past Florida and up the eastern coast of North America. This was **valuable** knowledge. Catching the Gulf Stream made it easier for ships to travel from the Caribbean Sea to Europe.

After discovering the Gulf Stream, Ponce de León continued south, past modern-day Palm Beach, Fort Lauderdale, and Miami. He sailed around southern Florida, and on June 3, he turned north and began traveling up the coast of western Florida. When he saw Indian villages he went ashore to ask about the Fountain of Youth. None of the Florida Indians had ever heard of it. At some of the villages, he and his men got into fights with the Indians. By June 24, he stopped looking for the fountain and sailed away from Florida.

Yucatán

After he left Florida, Juan Ponce de León sailed southwest toward Cuba. On June 26, 1513, he and his men found land. Most of them thought it was part of Cuba. Instead the land was most likely the Yucatán **Peninsula** in southern Mexico. They sailed along the coast for two days, then went ashore to mend their sails. The Spaniards most likely landed between modern-day Cabo Catoche and Progreso.

On August 6, Ponce de León sailed east. He then sailed north of Cuba and caught the Gulf Stream currents. On August 18, he reached Eleuthera, one of the islands in the Bahamas. From there Ponce de León headed back to Puerto Rico with two of his ships. Anton de Alaminos, his pilot, or the person who **steered** the ship and kept track of where the ship went, continued to search the Bahamas for Bimini and the Fountain of Youth. The Fountain of Youth was never found.

 The Mayan Indians, who lived on the Yucatán Peninsula, built a walled city that was later called Tulum. This city was most active from 1200 to 1500. When Ponce de León sailed along the coast of the Yucatán Peninsula in 1513, he may have seen Tulum. This modern photograph shows what is left of Tulum today.

 This astrolabe was made in 1555. Sailors used astrolabes to judge how far north or south they were. A part of the astrolabe was lined up with the Sun during the day and with the North Star at night to guess the ship's position.

Five years after Ponce de León landed on the Yucatán Peninsula, Juan de Grijalba was given credit for being the first European to discover Mexico. Credit is the honor that someone who does something special gets. Grijalba's pilot on his 1518 voyage was Anton de Alaminos, who had been Ponce de León's pilot as well.

A Second Voyage to Florida

In early 1514, Juan Ponce de León sailed to Spain to report to King Ferdinand on his voyage. He received his second royal grant on September 27, 1514, which allowed him to colonize "the island of Florida which you discovered by Our command." From 1515 to 1518, Ponce de León went back and forth between Puerto Rico and Spain. He spent most of 1520 preparing for his second voyage to Florida. In February 1521, Ponce de León sailed for Florida. "I **intend** to discover more of the coast of the said Island and to learn if it is connected with [Mexico] or with some other land," he wrote to King Charles V, who ruled after King Ferdinand.

The **site** Ponce de León chose for his colony was on the west coast of Florida, probably near modern-day Fort Myers. In early July there was a battle with the Indians. The Spaniards were driven out of Florida. Ponce de León was badly wounded by an arrow in his thigh. He was taken to Havana, Cuba, where he died. He was 47 years old.

Timeline

Around 1474: Juan Ponce de León is born in Tervas de San Campos, Spain.

1493: He sails to Hispaniola with Christopher Columbus.

1502: Ponce de León returns to Hispaniola. He marries Leonor.

1503: Ponce de León takes part in a campaign against the Taíno Indians in Higüey, Hispaniola.

1504: He plays a big part in a second campaign against the Taínos, which ends in a massacre. He is named frontier governor of Higüey.

1506: Ponce de León travels to Puerto Rico to see if it is a good site for a colony.

1508: He starts a colony in Puerto Rico and becomes its first governor.

1511: There is a revolt of the Taíno Indians of Puerto Rico.

1513: Ponce de León discovers Florida, the Gulf Stream, and Mexico.

1514: He travels to Spain to report to King Ferdinand.

1515: He returns to Puerto Rico.

1516: Ponce de León travels back to Spain after King Ferdinand dies.

1518: He returns to Puerto Rico.

1521: Ponce de León sails to Florida to start a colony. In a battle with Indians, he is wounded. He is taken to Havana, Cuba, where he dies.

 After Ponce de León was wounded in battle, his soldiers carried him to a ship. He was taken to Havana, Cuba, where he died.

Remembering Ponce de León

Juan Ponce de León may be the only explorer who is more famous for what he did not find, the Fountain of Youth, than for what he did. Ponce de León's discoveries of Florida, the Gulf Stream, and Mexico were important.

Ponce de León may not have been the first European to get to Florida. However, he is the person who made it known that Florida existed. With his discovery of Mexico, it was the other way around. He was probably the first European to reach it. Ponce de León did not realize how valuable Mexico was though, and Juan de Grijalba later made the discovery known.

The Gulf Stream was Ponce de León's discovery in every way. He was the first person to notice it. He was also the first person to let the world know how useful those strong currents could be for Europeans sailing from the New World to Europe. Sailors would continue traveling along the Gulf Stream in the centuries to come.

Glossary

campaign (kam-PAYN) A plan to get a certain result, such as to win a battle.

conquered (KON-kerd) Overcame something, or took it over completely.

court (KORT) The king or queen's advisers and officers. Also a place where a royal family and the people surrounding a royal family live.

defeat (dih-FEET) To win against someone in a game or battle.

demands (dih-MANDZ) Appeals or orders given by a person or a group to another person or group.

diseases (dih-ZEEZ-ez) Illnesses or sicknesses.

fort (FORT) A strong building or place that can be guarded against an enemy.

Fountain of Youth (FOWN-tun UV YOOTH) A natural spring that was said to bring youth to anyone who drank from it.

frontier (frun-TEER) Having to do with the edge of a settled country, where the wilderness begins.

grants (GRANTS) Legal documents that give the holder ownership of a set piece of land.

intend (in-TEND) To plan or choose to do something.

lieutenants (loo-TEH-nents) People with a certain rank in the military.

massacre (MA-sih-ker) The act of killing a large number of people or animals.

nobles (NOH-bulz) People who belong to royalty or have a high rank.

page (PAYJ) A boy who works as an assistant to a knight, or a young man who works at the royal court.

peninsula (peh-NIN-suh-luh) An area of land surrounded by water on three sides.

replace (rih-PLAYS) To take the place of something with something else.

revolted (rih-VOLT-ed) To have fought or to have rebelled against someone or against a government.

settlers (SET-lerz) People who move to a new land to live.

site (SYT) The place where a certain event happens.

steered (STEERD) To have moved or guided something from one place to another.

valuable (VAL-yoo-bul) Important, or worth a lot of money.

voyage (VOY-ij) A journey, especially by water.

Index

Web Sites

Due to the changing nature of Internet links, PowerKids Press has developed an online list of Web sites related to the subject of this book. This site is updated regularly. Please use this link to access the list.
www.powerkidslinks.com/pslfe/deleon/

Primary Sources

Page 6. Left. The Construction of La Navidad. Woodcut. From Columbus' Letters. 1494. Published by Johann Bergmann in Basel. Osher Map Library, University of Southern Maine, Portland, Maine. **Page 6. Right.** Native Americans (*detail*). Hand-colored woodcut. 1505. German. Spencer Collection, New York Public Library, New York, NY. **Page. 9. Top.** Cave Painting. Early 1500s. Jose Maria Cave, East National Park, Dominican Republic. Jose Maria Cave has over 1,200 cave paintings made by the Taíno Indians. **Page 9. Bottom.** Dogs Attacking Indians (*detail*). Engraving. Circa 1594–1596. From Theodore de Bry's edition of Girolamo Benzoni's *La Historia del Mondo Nuovo* (Italian for *The History of the New World*). **Page 10. Top.** *Bananas and Other Fruit Trees of Hispaniola* (detail). Hand-colored woodcut. 1572. Based on a sketch by Girolamo Benzoni. Benzoni lived in the Caribbean and South America from 1541 to 1556. **Page 10. Bottom.** Map of the Caribbean (*detail*). 1511. By Peter Martyr (the English name of Pietro Martire d'Anghiera). Rare Book & Special Collections Division, Library of Congress, Washington D.C. **Page 12. Top.** Indians Dropping Salcedo into the River (*detail*). 1500s. From America, Benzoni Section, Part IV. By Theodore de Bry. **Page 12. Bottom.** Report of the Distribution of the First Gold Found on San Juan Island. 1510. The report lists how much gold each person got after the king's fifth was set aside. **Page 15. Top.** The First Capitulation for the Discovery of Bimini. Signed in Burgos, Spain, on February 23, 1512, by Ferdinand, king of Spain, and the Bishop of Palencia. **Page 19. Top.** Astrolabe. Bronze. 1555. Portuguese.